8 95

discarded

THE AMAZING FACT BOOK OF

BALLOONS

by PETER MARRIOTT

Illustrated by
JOHN BAVOSI and TOM BRITTAIN

A & P/Creative Education

J 623.74
Ma

The Chinese were the pioneers of the air. Nearly 2,000 years ago they invented the kite. We do not know for certain if this wonderful balloon existed, but it is possible.

21,561

Contents

A & P BOOKS
8105 Edgewater Dr.
Oakland, CA 94621
A division of
The Atlantic & Pacific Commerce Co., Inc.

Library of Congress Catalog Card No. 80−65592
Illustrations Copyright © 1973 The Archon Press Limited
Text Copyright © 1979 Franklin Watts Limited
First published in USA by A & P Books 1980
Hardbound edition distributed by Creative Education, Inc., Mankato, MN

ISBN 0−86550−008−8 Hardbound (Volume 5)
ISBN 0−86550−009−6 Softbound (Volume 5)
ISBN 0−86550−024−X Hardbound (12 Volume Set)
ISBN 0−86550−024−8 Softbound (12 Volume Set)

Printed in USA by Worzalla Publishing Co.

Introduction

People had dreamed of flying from the earliest times. They were jealous of the freedom and beauty of the birds. Over many centuries people had tried to fly like the birds by using flapping wings, but none of them succeeded. As the knowledge of science increased, it was learned that the air was made up of gases which had weight. It was also discovered that some gases were lighter than the gases in the air and would rise. Air heated over a fire would also rise as it expanded. These gases could be contained in light bags if the bags were lined or varnished. All of these ideas were brought together by the first balloonists – the Montgolfiers, who used heated air, and J. A. C. Charles who used hydrogen (a gas that is about fourteen times lighter than air). Their balloons were no more than frail bags of gas from which they suspended a basket to carry passengers.

There was still much to be learned as these aeronauts piloted their elegant craft into the skies for the first time. Many weird and wonderful balloons were constructed, some of which were more practical than others. Most of these early pioneers were French. Soon, great showmen travelled the world, amazing enormous crowds with their spectacular ascents. The balloon was even taken to war.

The early balloons were dependent on the unreliable winds to carry them along. The next great advance came with the development of engines which, for the first time, allowed the balloons to travel independently of the wind. The age of the giant passenger airships, like the gigantic *Graf Zeppelin,* had arrived. Not all of the problems had been solved, however, and a number of disasters to these airships, together with the arrival of faster winged airplanes, meant an end to their brief glory.

Today, balloons are used for sport and high-altitude studies. The development of materials and technology (including the availability of a safe lifting gas – helium) has renewed the interest in the use of airships for carrying passengers and cargo. The greatest age of ballooning may be yet to come.

In this book you will find some of the amazing balloons which made history with their successes or failures. They are all proof of man's inventive abilities and sense of adventure.

The Balloon:
The Montgolfier brothers' balloon was made of cotton cloth painted blue and lined with paper. (The Montgolfiers owned a paper mill at Annonay in France.) The balloon was 13.3 m (43.5 ft) in diameter. It was open at one end and filled with a "gas" made from burning chopped straw and wool. It was only later realized that this lifting "gas" was only hot air.

Montgolfier Balloon

The Montgolfier brothers, Etienne and Joseph, made history by launching the world's first passenger-carrying balloon. Early in 1783 the Montgolfiers demonstrated a model of their hot-air balloon. On 19 September 1783 a cock, a duck and a sheep became the first balloonists.

The First Passengers:
The cock, duck and sheep were carried in a basket suspended below the balloon. This first ascent was a great State occasion. King Louis XVI and his court watched the balloon rise from the ground at the Palace of Versailles. The animals landed safely about 3 km (2 miles) away.

First Manned Balloon

The unknown skies held great fears for man. King Louis XVI would not, at first, allow the Montgolfier brothers to build a balloon to carry men. He agreed to allow it only if the first aeronauts were criminals! On the remote chance that they returned alive, they would be given a free pardon. However, the King was persuaded to change his mind and on 15 October 1783 a young scientist, Francis Pilâtre de Rozier made the first manned ascent (although the balloon was attached to the ground).

The First Aeronauts:
On the first free flight at 1.54 pm on 21 November 1783, Pilâtre de Rozier and the Marquis d'Arlandes rose into the sky. The balloon climbed to about 90 m (300 ft) and drifted in the wind towards the River Seine. The balloon travelled 8 km (5 miles) before landing safely.
At one point the balloon fabric caught fire, but the aeronauts were able to put out the flames with the damp sponges they had brought along. The balloon was 15 m (49 ft) in diameter.

The Globe

At the same time as Etienne and Joseph Montgolfier were working on their hot-air balloons, another Frenchman, J. A. C. Charles, was experimenting with hydrogen balloons. Less than two months after the first man-carrying hot-air balloon flight Charles and Marie-Noël Robert made a flight of 33 km (20 miles) in the elegant red and gold *Globe*.

La Minerve

As the interest in ballooning grew at the end of the eighteenth century, many grand and eccentric balloons were designed. None could have been more ambitious than this incredible balloon designed by Etienne Robertson in 1804.

Robertson was a well-known showman at the beginning of the nineteenth century. He amazed audiences with his early slide-shows and magical tricks. He had made balloon ascents and told astounding stories of his exploits.

La Minerve was to be capable of taking a crew of sixty outstanding scientists on a voyage across the world, lasting over six months. The balloon was designed like a galleon with a large, 46 m (150 ft) diameter, hot-air filled bag in the place of its main sails. It was to have studios for music and study, conference and games rooms and even a church. There would be separate quarters for the women members of the expedition. Suspended below the galleon and reached by long silk ladders were to be a large barrel-shaped food and water store, an exercise room, a medicine room, and cupboards.

The balloon was to be propelled by a jet of hot air.

La Minerve would announce its arrival at ports of call by firing a cannon. The crew would then descend in smaller balloons which were towed behind it.

The design of this balloon was totally impractical and it is doubtful if even Robertson believed it could have flown. It was never built.

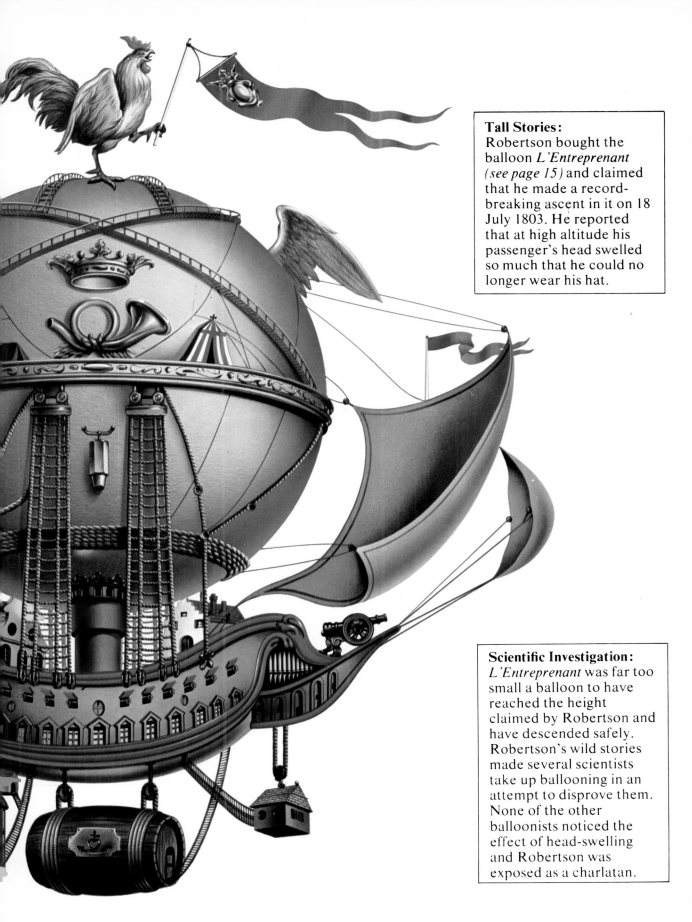

Tall Stories:
Robertson bought the balloon *L'Entreprenant* (*see page 15*) and claimed that he made a record-breaking ascent in it on 18 July 1803. He reported that at high altitude his passenger's head swelled so much that he could no longer wear his hat.

Scientific Investigation:
L'Entreprenant was far too small a balloon to have reached the height claimed by Robertson and have descended safely. Robertson's wild stories made several scientists take up ballooning in an attempt to disprove them. None of the other balloonists noticed the effect of head-swelling and Robertson was exposed as a charlatan.

Adorne's Montgolfière

Following the success of the early balloon flights, many other attempts were made. Most of these balloons were copies of the first Montgolfier balloons. In May 1784 Adorne was the first German to attempt an ascent. Unfortunately, his balloon crashed onto a roof and Adorne and his partner were seriously injured.

Balloonomania:
The success of the French balloonists led to a wave of ballooning attempts from other countries. Some of these early balloons were *Montgolfières* because they were easier to build and inflate than the hydrogen balloons. The first balloon ascent in Italy took place in February 1784. The first woman balloonist ascended in France in June 1784. In Austria the first ascent was in July (although the balloon was tethered), and in Britain in September 1784. The first successful ascent in Germany took place in October 1785.

Hydrogen Balloon

The first aeronaut in Britain was an Italian – Vincenzo Lunardi. Lunardi, a great showman, made many successful ascents before huge crowds. One of his elegant hydrogen balloons was decorated with a Union Jack in honor of his adopted country.

Napoleon's Coronation Balloon

The First Parachute Jump:
On 22 October 1797
André Garnerin made the
first successful descent by
parachute. He rose to
1000 m (3000 ft) in the
basket of the parachute,
which was suspended
beneath a hydrogen
balloon. Then he cut the
suspension cord and
descended safely.

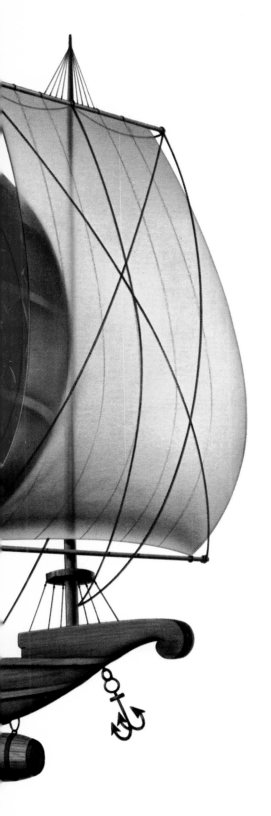

The celebration in Paris of the crowning of Emperor Napoleon Bonaparte in December 1804 was to be a very grand affair. Included in the festivities was a mammoth display of fireworks showing Napoleon's victories. At the height of the display a beautiful gold-painted balloon was released. The large unmanned balloon rose into the night skies above Paris and sailed majestically out of sight. It was a huge success.

Twenty-two hours later the balloon was over Rome – about 960 km (600 miles) away! A freak wind had carried the balloon across the French and Italian countrysides. It was reported that the balloon barely missed the dome of St Peter, and the Vatican. It then descended on the tomb of Nero, before finally disappearing into Lake Bracciano. The Italian press made much of this story, which the French found extremely embarrassing. The balloon was rescued from the lake and kept in the vaults of the Vatican.

The designer of the balloon was André Garnerin who had thrilled the Parisian crowds with great balloon and parachute feats. Garnerin had realized that ballooning was easier at night when there was less disturbance of the air. He took part in many spectacular ascents with balloons lit by fireworks and candles. He was a great showman and performed all over Europe. After the incident at Napoleon's coronation, Garnerin fell out of favor. His place was taken by the first female professional aeronaut, Madame Blanchard. Madame Blanchard would ascend in her balloon, trailing streams of fireworks, some of which she dropped on parachutes. All this was performed to the accompaniment of a large orchestra. Unfortunately, at a performance at the Tivoli Gardens in 1819, her balloon caught fire, she crashed into a house and fell to her death.

The First Channel-crossing Balloon

Designed by the Frenchman, Jean-Pierre Blanchard, this balloon was equipped with oars and a rudder. He hoped these would give him control of its direction and speed. With his American sponsor, Dr John Jeffries, he made the first successful crossing of the English Channel on 7 January 1785. As they approached the French coast, they were so near the water that most of their clothes had to be thrown overboard to lighten the balloon.

Wind-blown:
Blanchard's balloon was at the mercy of the wind. Its large gas bag acted as a sail. Several early balloonists fitted oars in the belief that they would be able to row against the wind, but they were not powerful enough. Blanchard's balloon lost so much altitude during the sea crossing that the crew had to throw the oars, rudder and silk decorations overboard. Eventually even their coats and boots, and Blanchard's trousers were thrown out of the gondola!

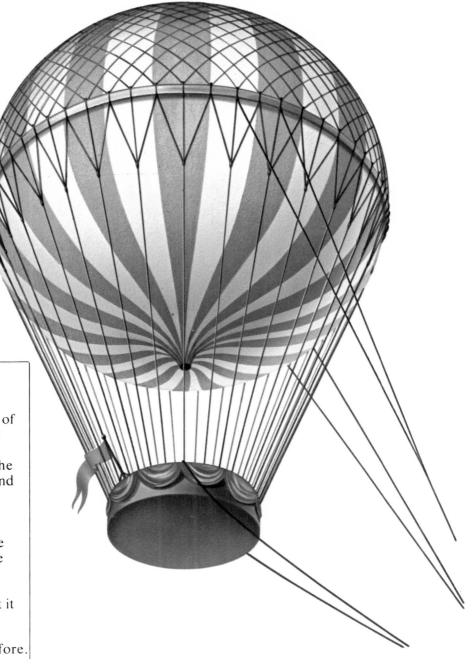

First Air Force:
Balloons allowed man to
see the countryside for
miles around.
Coutelle and Conté were
commissioned into the
first Air Force. The
balloon saw action at the
Battle of Fleurus in 1794.

L'Entreprenant

Two French scientists, Jean Marie Joseph
Coutelle and Nicolas Jacques Conté, realized that
balloons could be used in war. A captive balloon
(one held to the ground by ropes) made an ideal
observation platform from which artillery could
be directed.

Four-ballooned Airship

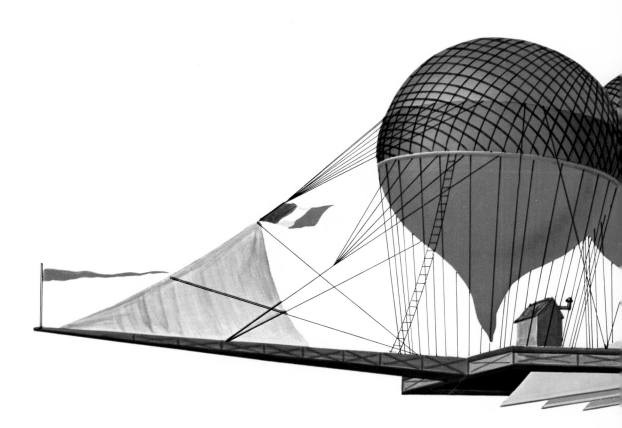

This wonderful four-ballooned giant airship was the idea of a Frenchman, Ernest Pétin. It looked like a sailing ship with balloons instead of sails. It was one of many airships designed in the middle of the nineteenth century which were meant to allow their crews control over their direction and speed. In this design the movable flat vanes (boards) below the balloons were meant to act as sails. They would allow the airship to travel at an angle to the wind like a sea-going ship. Four balloons were used as they would be less at the mercy of the wind than one immense balloon, as in the designs for *La Minerve*.

16

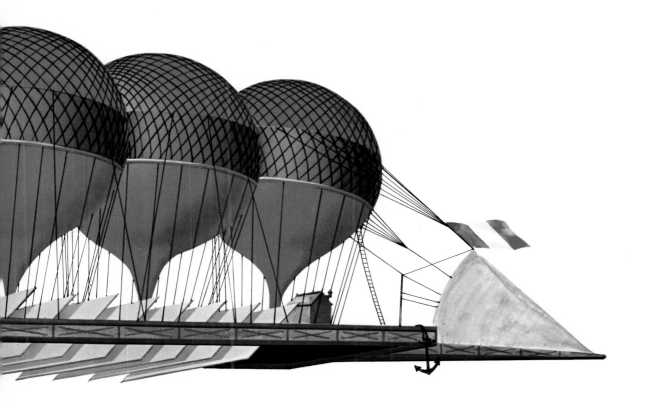

A large balloon takes enormous amounts of hydrogen gas. The usual method of manufacturing hydrogen gas in the 1800s was to mix dilute sulphuric acid with iron and zinc filings in a boiler. A chemical reaction took place and hydrogen gas was given off. This gas was then dried to remove water vapor, and any excess acid was removed. Early hydrogen generators were very slow and a large balloon could take days to fill. The balloon itself had to be varnished so that the gas would not pass straight through the fabric. If this happened, the balloon would lose gas faster than it was being put in.

Lighter Than Air:
Hydrogen gas was discovered by Henry Cavendish in 1766. This gas is much lighter than air and a balloon filled with it will rise. Hydrogen is a very inflammable gas and burns easily in the atmosphere. In certain mixtures with air it can even explode. Inflammable air, as it was originally known, had to be handled carefully.

Horse-carrying Charlière

Balloon shapes:
Early balloons had been globular, because this shape held most gas in the least fabric. As we have seen, they were impossible to control. The elongated balloon was less affected by the wind. Later powered airships all had this shape.

The showmen at the end of the eighteenth century had to make more and more daring ascents to keep the interest of the public. Pierre Tetu-Brissy decided to make an ascent on horseback to astonish the crowds. On 16 October 1798 Tetu-Brissy made his first successful ascent. The horse did not seem to be too upset by the experience. Not to be outdone, other showmen also made ascents on horseback and even took wild animals into the air.

The Atlantic

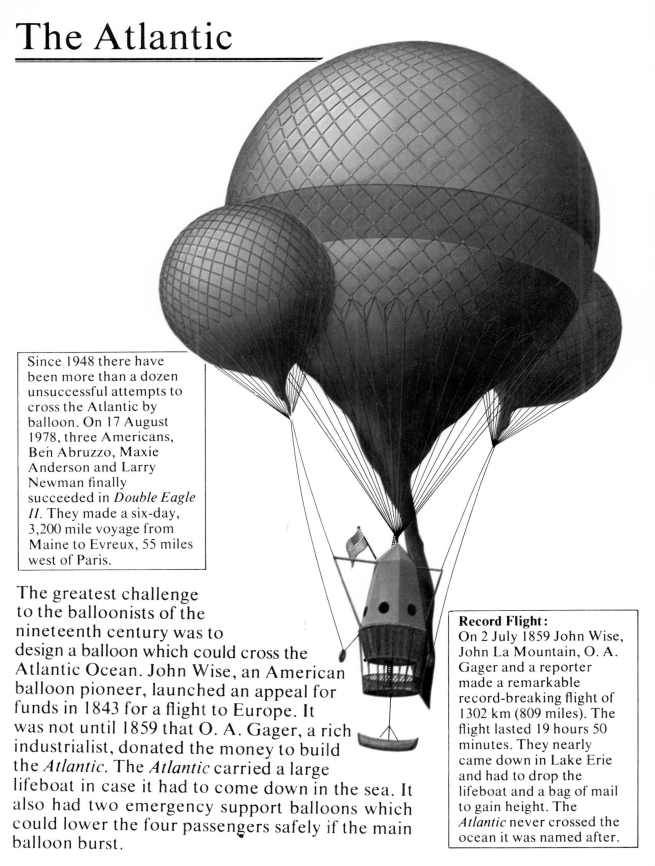

Since 1948 there have been more than a dozen unsuccessful attempts to cross the Atlantic by balloon. On 17 August 1978, three Americans, Ben Abruzzo, Maxie Anderson and Larry Newman finally succeeded in *Double Eagle II*. They made a six-day, 3,200 mile voyage from Maine to Evreux, 55 miles west of Paris.

The greatest challenge to the balloonists of the nineteenth century was to design a balloon which could cross the Atlantic Ocean. John Wise, an American balloon pioneer, launched an appeal for funds in 1843 for a flight to Europe. It was not until 1859 that O. A. Gager, a rich industrialist, donated the money to build the *Atlantic*. The *Atlantic* carried a large lifeboat in case it had to come down in the sea. It also had two emergency support balloons which could lower the four passengers safely if the main balloon burst.

Record Flight:
On 2 July 1859 John Wise, John La Mountain, O. A. Gager and a reporter made a remarkable record-breaking flight of 1302 km (809 miles). The flight lasted 19 hours 50 minutes. They nearly came down in Lake Erie and had to drop the lifeboat and a bag of mail to gain height. The *Atlantic* never crossed the ocean it was named after.

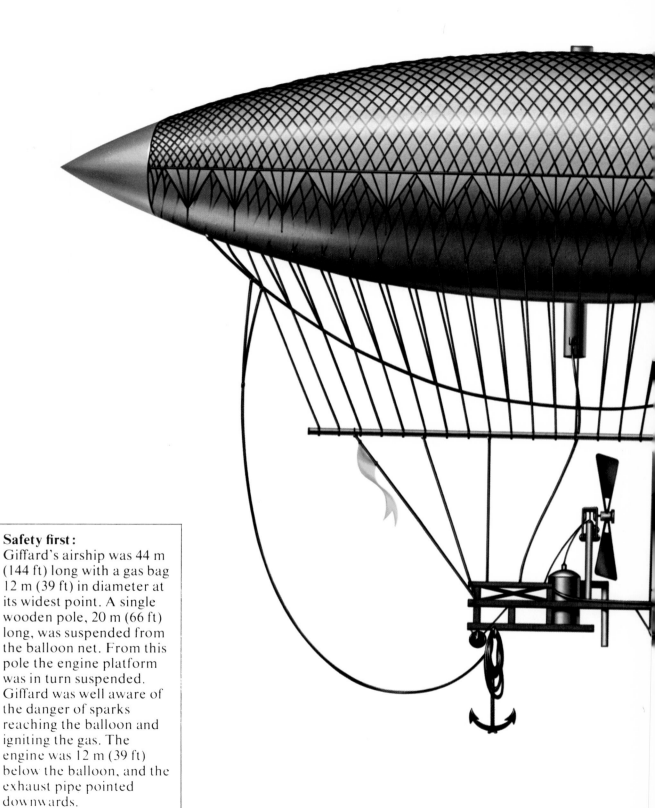

Safety first:
Giffard's airship was 44 m (144 ft) long with a gas bag 12 m (39 ft) in diameter at its widest point. A single wooden pole, 20 m (66 ft) long, was suspended from the balloon net. From this pole the engine platform was in turn suspended. Giffard was well aware of the danger of sparks reaching the balloon and igniting the gas. The engine was 12 m (39 ft) below the balloon, and the exhaust pipe pointed downwards.

First Steam-driven Airship

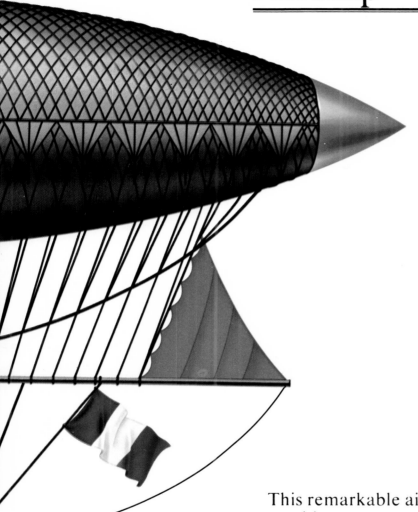

This remarkable airship was the first flying machine to use an engine. On 24 September 1852 Henri Giffard, the designer, took off on the first powered flight. Properly dressed in frock coat and top hat, Giffard stood on the small platform in front of the engine. The airship was able to carry 250 kg (552 lb) of coke and water to fuel the small steam engine. On the perfectly calm day the airship travelled 27 km (17 miles) at a speed of 8 k.p.h. (5 m.p.h.). The cigar-shaped balloon was pointed at both ends to reduce the resistance of the air. However, the steam engine was still not strong enough to steer Giffard's airship against even the slightest wind.

Man-powered Airship

This incredible airship was designed by a naval engineer, Henri Dupuy de Lôme. It was to be used by the French navy during the Franco-Prussian war. However, there were so many problems that the war was over before the airship could be completed. On its first flight in 1872 the eight sailors in the gondola managed to turn the large four-blade propeller fast enough to give the airship a speed of 8 k.p.h. (5 m.p.h.) over a short distance in calm conditions. It was realized that the sailors would never be able to give the airship enough power and the whole plan was scrapped. The sailor-powered airship never flew again.

Powered Flight:
Inventions and improvements in technology meant that new sources of power were becoming available. First came the steam engine as used in Giffard's balloon (page 21), but this was heavy and inefficient. In 1872 the Austrian Paul Haenlein made the first flight, using a gas engine. Several airships used electric motors.

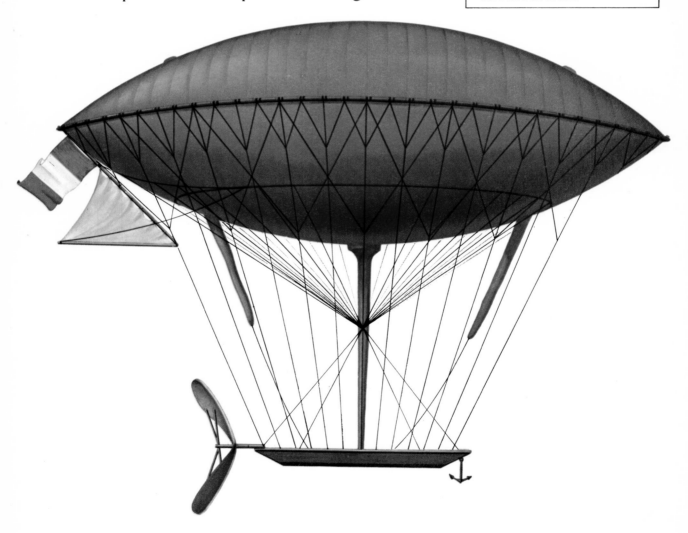

Drachen

German Skill:
The development of stabilizers was important for the future of airships. The *Drachen's* clever design showed the increasing knowledge of balloon design, which allowed the Germans to take over from the British as the most successful ballooning nation at the start of the twentieth century. The French specialized in tethered kite balloons.

In a high wind a captive balloon like *L'Entreprenant* (*see* page 15) would bob and weave about dangerously, and make observation difficult. This German balloon got over the problem by being part balloon and part kite. The long open bag at the end of the balloon filled with air and acted as a stabilizer. Even in a gusting gale the observation basket would remain steady and the kite-balloon would tilt into or out of the wind. Designed by Major von Parseval and Captain von Sigsfeld, *Drachen* (the Dragon) was built in 1896. This balloon was used until the end of the First World War.

La France

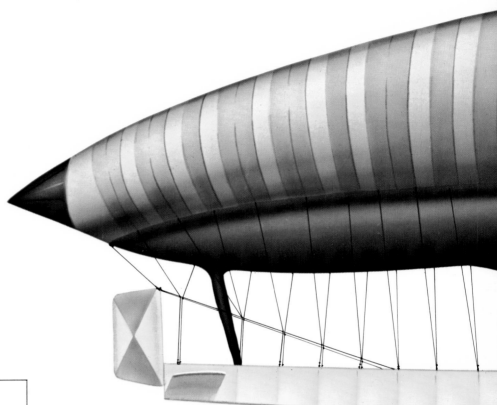

The Dirigibles:
La France was 50.4 m (164 ft) long with a maximum diameter of 8.4 m (27 ft). A long, narrow car, made out of bamboo and covered with canvas and silk, was slung underneath. The car contained lightweight batteries to power the 8 h.p. electric motor. The airship had a maximum speed of 23 k.p.h. (14 m.p.h.). The French gave the name "dirigible", meaning "able to be navigated", to this craft. Since then the word "dirigible" has been used to describe airships.

The elegant *La France* was the first truly navigable (steerable) airship. On 9 August 1884 this long and slender airship was piloted on a figure-of-eight course of 8 km (5 miles), returning to its starting point. The designers of *La France*, two French army engineers, Charles Renard and Authius Krebs, had begun work on the airship in 1878. The failure of Dupuy de Lôme's man-powered airship (*see* page 22) made the French government reluctant to support the project. Eventually Léon Gambetta, a leading French politician who had escaped from the siege of Paris by balloon, gave them the £8,000 needed.

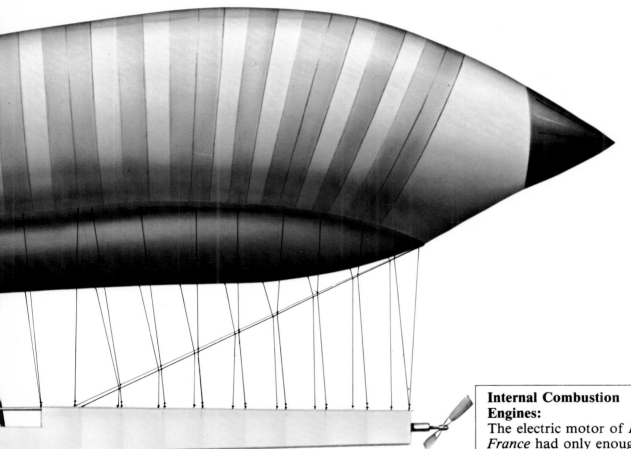

The completed airship took off from the parade ground at Chalais-Meudon at 4 p.m. on a calm evening. As soon as they were clear of the trees, the two aeronauts switched on the motor and headed slowly south. They soon found that the airship responded to the controls and were able to turn to the west. Later they turned the airship around and returned to their starting point.

The flight, which lasted twenty-three minutes, was the first in which the aeronauts were truly in control. However, *La France* was only fast enough to steer in the lightest of winds.

Internal Combustion Engines:
The electric motor of *La France* had only enough power for short, slow journeys on calm days. Giffard's steam-powered airship had been even slower. A more efficient and lighter source of power was needed if airships were to become practical. In the year after the first flight of *La France* a German engineer called Gottlieb Daimler designed the first gasoline-driven internal combustion engine. This much more efficient source of power was to make the future of airships certain.

Captive Balloon

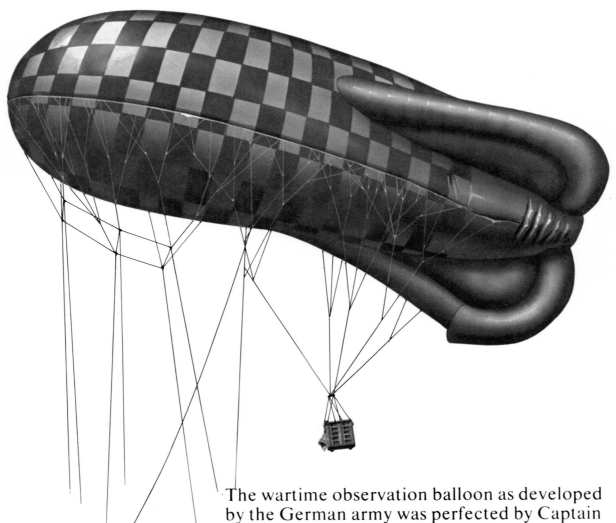

Barrage Balloons:
During both the World Wars captive balloons, very similar in design to these, were used to defend cities from attack by enemy aircraft and missiles. An effective barrage (barrier) against attack was formed by lines of balloons.

The wartime observation balloon as developed by the German army was perfected by Captain Albert Caquot of the French army. These beautifully designed balloons were able to remain steady in even the worst conditions. Developed during the First World War, these balloons faced a new problem – enemy aircraft. The captive balloon was a sitting target for the enemy fighter planes. Captain Caquot issued his observation crews with parachutes so they could jump from their balloons at the first sign of danger. He also developed a motorized winch which could rapidly haul the balloon down to the ground.

Meteorological Balloon

In order to have an accurate forecast of the weather we need to know the conditions high in the atmosphere as well as on the ground. Airline pilots also need to know the conditions they will be flying in. This ingenious meteorological balloon is designed to provide this information cheaply.

The balloon is filled with hydrogen and rises into the atmosphere. Beneath the balloon is a suspended package containing a radio transmitter and instruments to measure pressure, humidity (the amount of moisture in the atmosphere) and temperature. The transmitter converts the readings into signals which it sends back to observers on the ground. The transmitter aerial is above the instrument package and also serves as a radar "reflector". This reflector is designed to show up easily on radar screens and is used to record the movements of the balloon. This gives a record of the high altitude wind direction and speed.

When the balloon has served its purpose and risen to a height of between 20 and 35 km (12 to 21 miles) it is released and the instruments parachute back to Earth where they can be used again.

Graf Zeppelin

The enormous *Graf Zeppelin* was the world's most successful airship. Launched in 1928 this passenger-carrying airship made a round-the-world flight in 1929. The airship took off from Lakehurst, New Jersey on 8 August returning 21 days and 7 hours later. The captain of the *Graf Zeppelin* was Dr Hugo Eckener. The *Graf Zeppelin* was named after Count (Graf) Ferdinand von Zeppelin. Zeppelin was an army officer who was determined that Germany should have airships to rival those of the French. He believed that airships were the major weapons of any future war. His first airship flew on 2 July 1900 just before his sixty-second birthday. Eckener was a reporter covering this first flight. Later Eckener and Zeppelin formed the first passenger airline, carrying over 10,000 passengers before the First World War. During the war Zeppelin's airships made the first bombing raids on England.

Engines:
The engines of Zeppelin's first airship were two 15 h.p. Daimler engines, which could drive the airship at 26 km (16 miles) per hour. The *Graf Zeppelin* had five 550 h.p. Maybach engines mounted below the airship. These engines were able to drive this mammoth airship at 128 k.p.h. (79.6 m.p.h.).

Count Zeppelin died in 1917. After the war Germany was not allowed to build any more airships until 1928 when Eckener built the LZ127 and named it in honor of the Count. The *Graf Zeppelin* was over 235 meters (770 feet) long and weighed 117 tons. It had a crew of forty and carried twenty passengers. The gasbags contained in the rigid aluminum frame carried 104,700 cubic meters (3,700,000 cubic feet) of hydrogen. *Graf Zeppelin* crossed the Atlantic on its first long voyage in October 1928 and made its epic round-the-world trip one year later. In 1931 the *Graf Zeppelin* crossed the Arctic Circle and the same year, the pyramids of Egypt. Then the *Graf Zeppelin* settled down to make regular crossings between Germany and Brazil until it was retired in 1937. The *Graf Zeppelin* had carried over 13,000 passengers and travelled over 1,610,000 km (1,000,000 miles) without incident.

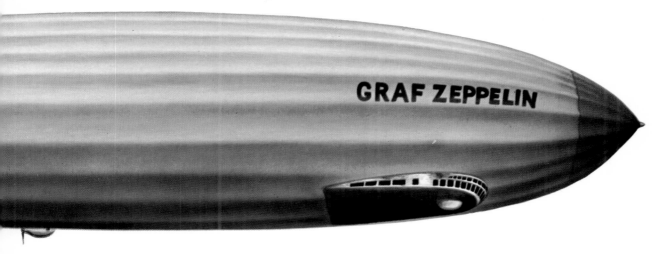

The ''Hindenburg'': In 1936 an even larger airship was built. This 200 ton monster carried 50 passengers. On 6 May 1937 the *Hindenburg* burst into flames while approaching Lakehurst. Thirty-six people were killed and this disaster marked the end of the age of the great airships.

Daffodil II

Since the early flights of the Montgolfier and Charles balloons, ballooning has been a challenge to man's sense of adventure. Today ballooning has become a popular sport. One great challenge is to reach higher and higher altitudes. *Daffodil II* is a beautifully designed hot-air balloon with which Julian Nott and Felix Pole from Britain captured the world altitude record for hot-air balloons on 24 January 1974. Taking off from Bhopal in central India, *Daffodil II* reached a height of 13,580 m (44,554 ft).

Balloon Records:
The world altitude record for hydrogen balloons is held by Commander D. Ross of the United States Navy Reserve, who reached an astounding 34,660 m (113,739·9 ft) on 4 May 1961. The world's largest hot-air balloon is the 14,158 cu m (5,000,000 cu ft) *Gerard A. Heineken*, which is capable of carrying 30 passengers in a two-tier gondola.

Glossary

aeronaut:	a balloon pilot.
airship:	a large balloon fitted with a means of propulsion.
altitude:	the height reached by a balloon.
captive ascent:	a balloon ascent made with the balloon tied to the ground with long ropes or cables.
Charlière:	a hydrogen balloon based on the original J. A. C. Charles' balloon.
free ascent:	a balloon ascent with no attachment to the ground.
gondola:	a basket (originally boat-shaped) suspended beneath a balloon and used to carry passengers. Nowadays "gondola" usually means the pressurized closed car of a high-altitude balloon.
meteorological balloon:	a balloon used to make observations of the weather.
Montgolfière:	a hot-air balloon modelled on the original Montgolfier balloon.